Date: 4/29/19

BR 627.8 BOW
Bowman, Chris,
Dams /

EVERYDAY ENGINEERING

Dams

by Chris Bowman

BELLWETHER MEDIA • MINNEAPOLIS, MN

Note to Librarians, Teachers, and Parents:

Blastoff! Readers are carefully developed by literacy experts and combine standards-based content with developmentally appropriate text.

Level 1 provides the most support through repetition of high-frequency words, light text, predictable sentence patterns, and strong visual support.

Level 2 offers early readers a bit more challenge through varied simple sentences, increased text load, and less repetition of high-frequency words.

Level 3 advances early-fluent readers toward fluency through increased text and concept load, less reliance on visuals, longer sentences, and more literary language.

Level 4 builds reading stamina by providing more text per page, increased use of punctuation, greater variation in sentence patterns, and increasingly challenging vocabulary.

Level 5 encourages children to move from "learning to read" to "reading to learn" by providing even more text, varied writing styles, and less familiar topics.

Whichever book is right for your reader, Blastoff! Readers are the perfect books to build confidence and encourage a love of reading that will last a lifetime!

This edition first published in 2019 by Bellwether Media, Inc.

No part of this publication may be reproduced in whole or in part without written permission of the publisher. For information regarding permission, write to Bellwether Media, Inc., Attention: Permissions Department, 6012 Blue Circle Drive, Minnetonka, MN 55343.

Library of Congress Cataloging-in-Publication Data

Names: Bowman, Chris, 1990- author.
Title: Dams / by Chris Bowman.
Description: Minneapolis, MN : Bellwether Media, Inc., 2019. | Series:
  Blastoff! Readers. Everyday Engineering | Includes bibliographical
  references and index. | Audience: Ages 5-8. | Audience: Grades K to 3.
Identifiers: LCCN 2018000217 (print) | LCCN 2018004969 (ebook) | ISBN
  9781626178229 (hardcover : alk. paper) | ISBN 9781681035635 (ebook)
Subjects: LCSH: Dams–Juvenile literature.
Classification: LCC TC541 (ebook) | LCC TC541 .B69 2019 (print) | DDC 627/.8–dc23
LC record available at https://lccn.loc.gov/2018000217

Editor: Paige V. Polinsky   Designer: Jeffrey Kollock

Printed in the United States of America, North Mankato, MN

Table of Contents

What Are Dams?

Dams stop or change
the flow of water.

They are usually built
along rivers and streams.

Early dams **irrigated** crops. They also stored drinking water.

Today, dams do this and more.
Some create paths for boats.

Many dams protect cities against floods. Others help make power.

mine

pollution

Sometimes dams are built near mines. They keep **pollution** from spreading.

Embankment dams are large hills of rocks and soil. Their clay centers keep water out.

Gravity dams use **concrete**. Their weight holds water back.

embankment dam

10

Three Gorges Dam

Location: Yangtze River; Hubei, China

Type: gravity dam

Year Completed: 2006

Engineer: Pan Jiazheng

Size:

length: 7,660 feet (2,335 meters)
height: 607 feet (185 meters)

supports

buttress dam

Buttress dams have extra **supports** along their walls.

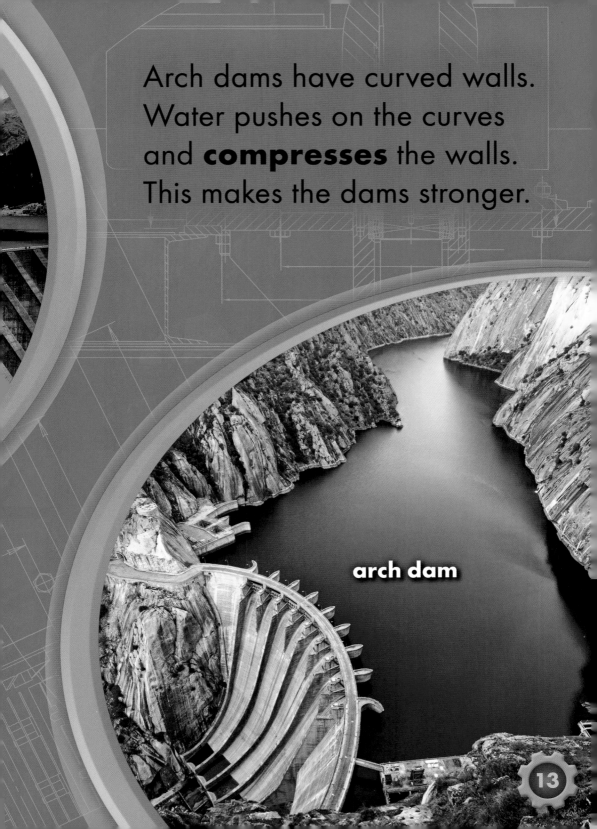

Arch dams have curved walls. Water pushes on the curves and **compresses** the walls. This makes the dams stronger.

arch dam

Hydropower at Work

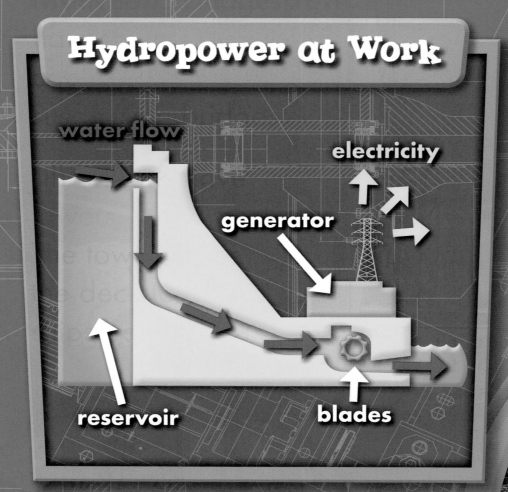

water flow

electricity

generator

reservoir

blades

Hydropower dams let some water through. The flowing water spins blades.

This powers machines called **generators**. They make **electricity**! Gravity or arch dams can be used for this.

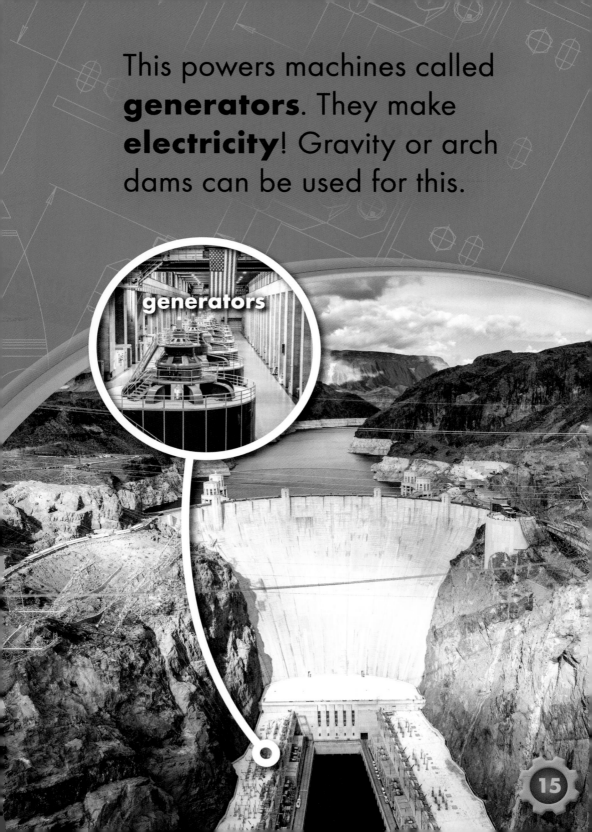

generators

How Do Dams Work?

Water presses against dams.
But **gravity** pushes the
dams into the ground.

Some dams hold water with their weight alone. Others have extra supports for strength.

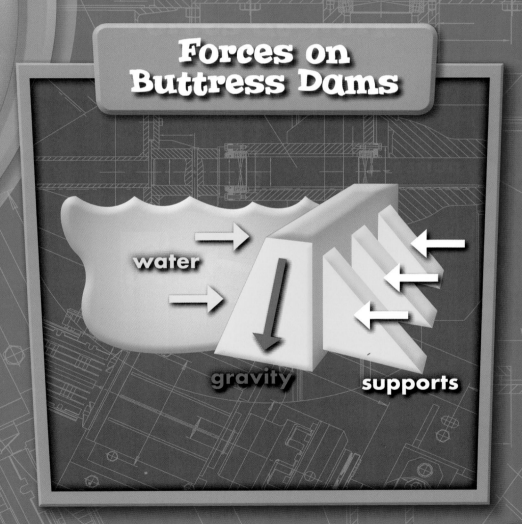

Forces on Buttress Dams

water

gravity

supports

Dams back water
into **reservoirs**.
Gates open and close
to control the water levels.

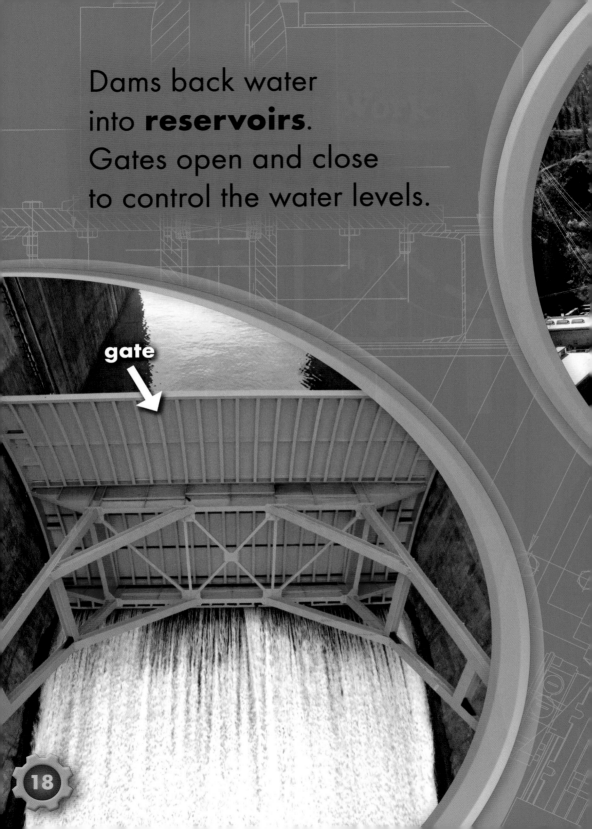

gate

spillway

Spillways are used for heavy rains. They send extra water downstream.

Today, fewer new dams are being built. But hydropower dams are still popular.

These **structures**
help power the world!

Glossary

compresses—pushes inward; this force is called compression.

concrete—a hard building material made of stone, cement, and water

electricity—energy used for power

generators—machines that create electricity

gravity—a force that pulls objects toward the ground

irrigated—sent water to other places for farming

pollution—harmful matter

reservoirs—man-made lakes

spillways—passages for extra water from a dam

structures—things that are built

supports—parts that help hold up a structure

To Learn More

AT THE LIBRARY
Loh-Hagan, Virginia. *Dams.* Ann Arbor, Mich.:
Cherry Lake Publishing, 2017.

Olson, Elsie. *Dams.* Minneapolis, Minn.:
Abdo Pub., 2017.

Sikkens, Crystal. *A Dam Holds Back.* New York, N.Y.:
Crabtree Publishing Company, 2017.

ON THE WEB
Learning more about
dams is as easy as 1, 2, 3.

1. Go to www.factsurfer.com.

2. Enter "dams" into the search box.

3. Click the "Surf" button and you will see a
   list of related web sites.

With factsurfer.com, finding more information is
just a click away.

Index

The images in this book are reproduced through the courtesy of: Pipochka, front cover; chrupka, front cover; NaMo Stock, front cover, pp. 2-3, 22-24; Bubushonok, front cover, pp. 4-24 (blueprint background); darin.k, pp. 4-24 (gears); Vitaly Fedotov, pp. 4-5; Pakenee Kittipinyowat, pp. 6-7; A.PAES, p. 7; SULEYMAN DOGAN, p. 8; David Wall/ Alamy, pp. 8-9; Martchan, p. 9 (inset); f8grapher, p. 10; gyn9037, pp. 10-11; Nicola Auckland, pp. 12-13; irakite, p. 13; okili77, p. 14; turtix, pp. 14-15; R Scapinello, p. 15 (inset); risteski goce, pp. 16-17; vichie81, p. 18; cathaus photography, pp. 18-19; saiko3p, pp. 20-21.